Weston's Unsent Letters to Modotti

Weston's Unsent Letters
to Modotti

Chad Parmenter

Tupelo Press
North Adams, Massachusetts

Weston's Unsent Letters to Modotti.
Copyright © 2015 Chad Parmenter. All rights reserved.

Library of Congress Catalog-in-Publication data available upon request.
ISBN: 978-1-936797-67-7

Cover and text designed by Bill Kuch.

Cover photograph of Tina Modotti: "The White Iris" (1921), by Edward Weston
(1886–1958). Platinum or palladium print, 24.1 × 19 cm. Johan Hagemeyer
Collection / CCP Accession number 76.5.27. Copyright © Center for Creative
Photography, The University of Arizona Foundation / Art Resource, NY. Used
with permission of Center for Creative Photography (www.creativephotography.
org), Artists Rights Society (ARS NY), and Art Resource (www.artres.com).

Title page photograph: "Mella's Typewriter or La Técnica" (1928), by Tina
Modotti (1896–1942). Gelatin-silver print, 9 ⅜ x 7 ½ inches. Copyright © The
Museum of Modern Art. Used with permission and licensed by SCALA / Art
Resource (www.artres.com).
First paperback edition: November 2015.

Tupelo Press is an award-winning independent literary press that publishes fine
fiction, nonfiction, and poetry in books that are a joy to hold as well as read.
Tupelo Press is a registered 501(c)(3) nonprofit organization, and we rely on
public support to carry out our mission of publishing extraordinary work that may
be outside the realm of the large commercial publishers. Financial donations are
welcome and are tax deductible.

"I am alone in this great room — no, you are with me, but only your counterpart on the wall, forming a kiss I never got."
　　　　　　　　—Edward Weston, to Tina Modotti

Contents

Weston's Unsent Letters to Modotti

Tina mia — this is the night after the night after
I, spherical aberration, blur in your world, left.
But I write to you, or, no, the you my gaze made —
naked frame for my broken-open core.

Not my patron sinner anymore, you crooned to me
"Vaya con nada camerado mia," already knowing I go
with nothing but sight — you meant "my friend,"
you said "my camera." I said "my light." My
words sounded strange to me then, as if someone
spoke for me.

You know there is no me — that "I" is a negative,
is an image of someone else.

Nowhere is the where we were — where I write you, at the end of the lens arc light makes in my — never our — darkroom. This is a negative of us — an Edward and Tina the world will never see, never developed into a picture. This was us in a more intimate fiction — the you made by my gaze, the me you made with yours.

But a body holds no story.

I'm erasing it from the glass face — a new window for my studio.

My gaze sits in it. And I can't find you.

But in that wash of the loss of us, what lushness.
The music fused it, fused us in just that thought-
dissolving kiss that brought me with you into the
country you made yours — where desert night, its
obsidian wind, ran a phantom skin down my skin,
and the cities glittered even in the noon sun —
where water's spirit haunted their searing air.

You wrote in a letter I got this morning, "the
pattern will be clearer to us I think after." It
will be, and we will remember us as photograph,
memory as dream in frame. And if you could take
me — into just that mask of just that past — I
would not need to feel it leaving me.

This dusk makes me think less of you — of your contours. Its lilac haze reframes the everyday — makes it strange. It husks the clouds above Glendale in an alien steel.

Now, I hear, in memory, *Eye of the adulterer watches for dusk* — that verse in a voice that must be my mother's, hushed, earnest as the burn of streetlights that shutter to life outside.

But, my one of many women, my something under love, I am only fully human looking into the dusk of the model's body as hazed by the lens — in its glow, in its pose, in its transubstantiation to the broken mask of a photograph. My love is of its hushed, blushing nothing.

Your blank look was too much a mask — too much soul
in it broken open. You, naked, were like broken
panes — in you, the lie of Cubism came home. The
conceptual would end when you laid there, bare,
your look a hood — the face of fetishization.

But it was the look I gave you — all I could take
of you. I take it back.

We were never in the same nation — even in Mexico.
I lived in one defined by my art — you have your
beloved people, the ones your own gaze shapes
among the Riveras and their compañeros. I could
get lost in a clay vase — you in the war to save
its maker.

I know you still go to the bull fights — I know
because I need to believe you're still you. And
I would ask you to shoot — with your best lens —
the Graflex — the white bull's dying moment — but
it would not be cold enough for me.

These lights I live by: the smallest aperture can capture — from afternoon — the monochrome of a good blood moon on tide, at night. The white sheets of palladium paper, though they will cost you, lend a texture to the nude that makes look a form of touch. You never saw them. You wanted sighs, not facts. But facts last.

There are the secrets that can only come from a teacher: just a touch of salt of iron, kissed with silver nitrate, will give an image the freshness of "yes." When you end a session, and the object or model seems to want more — do what art wants you to. Know that sight is its own — its own light.

9

The roses in your picture hold no core — no
center — though they mirror the frame a face is.
They are made of breaking away, like a face would
into a laugh, or into a look of some suffering
under love. They harmonize the shapes of naked
space with desert night — no shape, only a letting
go that can't be captured as picture. They need
the eye to view them into bloom.

If I gave you those roses — I may have made your
eye stray. Did I give them to you — it hurts too
much when I try to remember.

You are not the true artist — not of us two. You
feel too far into what you see. A photograph is
not of a subject — not even the death of it.
It is the thing itself — emulsion collected in
tranquility — or that lack of personality you have
too much of.

Becoming nothing — that is how we bring it into
view. I tried — with my vacant and vacating gaze —
to teach it into you.

There are no years or hours — and so there is no
vacant space — in still film, in the image that
fills it, in the vision that it incubates with its
chemical will. There is no incoherence of many
points of view — as Eliot says of Bergson's verse-
nervous words. These are the ones I believe I
love: *Love is making artificial objects — tools
to make tools.*

In the studio, as a tool of my own sight, I know no
buried life. There is only form, that can't dance,
lovely in its fixity, as free of need as me.

Your form — framed by my small hands, that you called "dangerous to know" — looked so like a fever dream of a tree to me. The truth of the universe is ruin — it insists — but out of the ruin the new — your core. I was never there.

The cypress on the broken rock overlook above the waves, where I find my wide eye flying, free of here, of us, holds — in its fire-scoured trunk — the likeness of fire and of our inner visions of outer space — hard stars, matte night, everything severing everything in its moving to be free.

She's the image you are but far more — more star-beautiful — and by that I mean mutable — Maria, Joan in "The Passion of Joan of Arc," scintillant with distance, giant, silent on the screen where I see her, leave her, am free from her. Her tears are not real. Yours were.

Remember you trembling and tender like white light on dark water — in the nest of shed clothes we used as a bed — shaking because of making love. I was making pictures in my mind — "I" is a picture-making of the mind — as far from you as film from the true Joan of Arc.

Look how her tears charge — carve away the dark of her face. Their torture of her makes her eyes shine gray with faith. Look how her power only grows in motion. Remember how you never moved — never moved me.

14

Sinematic — that's what film becomes in motion.
And it spins in the hunt of the stillness our art
lives in. But no one wants that light, its weight.

By "no one," I only mean me.

But perhaps I really see how cinema will kill
photography. Passion as action — written by light
like still film is — not as what they call art —
no — more its own source. More heart — or its
avatar.

Nothing but light comes in at the eye — Yeats told
us love does, but love is kindled in the lens.
There, the one you're taking takes you in, and
the image is the meeting of your beings — its charm
become a harmony.

I needed you to see through me. And only no one can.

A photograph is not a ghost or past. It is its
own. And you are yours now — or only ever were.

Now, at the hour when the bats are hunting above
your house — how many thousand miles from mine —
I find my poor, devoted Flora stored with the rest
of the negatives. In this one, she's a sort of
ghost, a memory of Eve — pale hand at a pale
apple, made like her of mist-thick light. The
leaves above her look like her eyes, blurred and
wind-burdened.

I see my new Eve, Charis, her paradise the
studio, her apple missing a white bite — in the
finished print, it will hold the same, strained
radiance of shade in a negative, of palladium
paper before the picture harvested its darknesses.

Sex was a lead lens — even for you — or the you
my gaze made — there was no looking through.
Search under what you want it to be, and there it
is — just the shutter of desire, and the vacancy
in us, lit up in an instant — an image abandoned
as soon as it was had.

You have been banished now, exiled from that
desert neverland, and from the myths I visioned
you into. Please be as free from desires as I am
immersed in them — temptless, depthless, given in.

This nude will be seen as the true you — Weston's best version of her — done from the azotea of our hacienda. If you could look again at that counter-part's eyes — shuttered against noon sun — full behind their lids as the rose bulbs that lit our darkroom — and your lips blistered kiss-black — you could tell me why your hands vanished under your perfect back, as if tied by desire.

Thighs I could still whisper apart — why did they lay so far outside my frame? But what a pretty, prison pattern radiates from that "her" — a lattice of cracks in the patio. And what a heart of dark hair at the root of her torso — here, in this negative, transfigured into some child of writing and lightning.

I will wash her from the glass — another window. This one will sit in my studio door.

You loved the tragedy factory of me — or I
imagined you did. But I never told you my story
in images — in the undone style of fire.

When fever burnt her — Mother — out of our lives,
I became frame-numb, engine, inhuman. I felt like
the look of my own breath — when Father let the
fire in our hearth die down. He could not will to
build it any more than meet my eyes. Hers were
in mine.

If Kodak had not outgrown them, I'd give you the
Bull's Eye he left on my bed then. Its case was
black and slick as a casket.

    It felt as cool as I knew her body would —
    free of her fever.

When I held it up and squinted into it — it squint-
ed into me — and there was nothing then but that
look. Not even one to do the looking. I felt that
with you — or wanted to.

Memory will be remade by our art — the camera
carried by anyone and seen as a way to drain past
out of the now. Past as fact. Past as mask.

There is no tender memory in me, so they shiver —
tremory — and break as pictures — as frames.
"I" was a negative, a camera you used.

When you had sat just once to me, I still saw
Modotti — only — the mode — cipher, "tiger-skinned
queen," the name you grew in your film, "The
Tiger's Coat." Your stills filled all the
magazines — for a fraction, a second, of how long
my images will stay.

Mine are yours — their letting go, their echo.
But no one will say that. They will filter my
pictures through theirs, and then they will
describe my eye.

Shut out of the cloud of the now — in my studio
— in this winter shiver — wind will develop a model
of the city in my mind, by sound and by scent — the
wash of exhaust, screened through trees, mirrors
your pictures' birth — salt of halite, salt of
iron — to bring me free of the shiver your negative
gives me.

    What did you give me — more than power over
all I might discover, there under your layers of
harem costume. You gave me fame — or its vacated
frame.

It is as if you're more me than a fixture — picture
— star with char-dark hair.

But you were bright as a tiger — brighter. In this
chill — I wish the burning of you hurt.

The savior who was yours before me — Richey — left
you in widowhood's shallow shadow. I like the
picture of him, fear-harrowed, Christ-like in his
eyes, how they look like they are looking a moment
open.

Your men, since me, have been Romantic, Marxist,
but with busy hearts. And I love to read of you
leaving them as I left you — like me — in exile.
I say they couldn't take your gaze — its radiant
weight.

> That's why Diego paints your hair over your
> eyes — a pour of artless tar — like night
>
> stifled inside a rose bud. As diffused as
> he needed you to be.

The rose bulb under the developer charges this
dark with the color of blush — of blood — of touch
as it develops into red on the touched one's skin.
Come home. Let mine in.

Who is your future this year? Picture — speak
to me.

Stay my gaze — its vacancy — in which I hide my
frame kind of life. Don't come back to me from
your pure corner of Europe — that afterlife of the
socialite socialists.

It incarnated a dark — not lady — a frame in which
the Modern wandered toward its birth, and that you,
nude as factory smoke, as a gear with its teeth
worn down — you hold the old world back in the art-
starving dark where its cares could not touch us.

And still this vision must not come undone.

Your star-dark look — transformed by my work —
woke me out of my Pictorial dreamtime — treelined,
streamlined by the portrait-maker's torque, the
painter's mania. I was them, then became the same
demon as machines and stones.

You were the best of the photographer's devils.
You were the helper who knew my mind — that vacant
space where images live.

I lost the one of you in mask and black dress —
when you were me, for El Dia de los Muertos — the
only self-portrait I could take. You looked like
dark made art. I mined that look — I still do —
and I leave you, blank, I-less, mine.

I write free of the here — where you are — in one
where the sea is bleached — negatized — by light —
just past violet, at that mechanized time of night.
I try to leave the nightmare in my studio behind
me — of my father, gun to his eye, you, nude, on
his knee.

      Critics liken my own eyes to gunsights.
Yours are more urgent — il miglior fabbro — your
art better-hearted. Mine has no soul. So it will
not die.

You don't remember my bright eyes — I don't. But I
do yours. Even here — in the dark, on the Point,
by myself — I see their innocent squint, their
hurt, and, in it, something dim — an image of me.

      I can't tell you how to use them — so I write
these notes knowing that — in art — I have made the
mistakes any camera can — with inhumanity.

It was never a matter of aperture — what speed of
what shutter — exact slant of this or that exact
light — or whatever living picture sits and waits
to be taken — to be made new. It was never about
pure work.

It was always this — photography as poetry, light
as writing, not what your eyes may take in, but
what you empty out of you, displaced by this
making, the order that chords and guides fire, and
the solder and voltage of Modern culture.

That's a negative's capability. That is this
art's. Make it yours.

And be unmade by it. And maybe then — be real
to me.

The public's eyes are flies' — there we are air,
splintered into different identities.

You'd adore this synthesis — of glitter into
water into glitter — like a film of heaven on
these colonies of plankton, their flares opal -
cold under the roughened surface — nervous as
house lights — living in moving.

Where you are — in the heaven of a negative, or
nowhere, or out of reach of me — or all three —
there is a scar that can be found only by your
own, hurt art. Lean to the lens. Breathless,
motionless, press in. Focus. Wait for it to
take on your own brightness.

Now breathe. Refresh your sight. The first kiss
of the light.

I took a picture for the you I never saw — the real one — but it would never have arrived before you died. Your counterpart — on the wall — can see it over my shoulder.

By what was once our piece of the sea, a pair of, are they ghost or stone crabs, as pale as ghost or stone — claws yawned bone tines, slowly fighting the stillness of the windless dawn.

> The camera's case — there where you were, where I crave a look at you now, the ghost I made with my own gaze — as if the case might be cracked — and you flash past.

They came undone — from each other — and waltzed underwater. The waves breaking on and darkening the rock — where I always wanted us to walk — or whatever of an "us" there was — the picture of them shattered in that wake.

This letter will never be sent — not because Tina has died — but because it's to you, the Tina made by my gaze. I never knew another. I wish I did. But even that wish comes shaped by my desire for you — the numb one.

Where what she was met my making gaze — are you there? That flash of shadow they made — I lived in it — in you — still do.

Look at — no — through me — and tell me who you see — who I am.

Notes

This sequence is intended to explore questions of technology, identity, and poetry using as a lens details from Edward Weston's life and relationships, especially with his relationship with the artist Tina Modotti. The poems are not meant as a guess about what Weston might have thought, felt, or said.

"Tina mia,"
"My words sounded strange to me then, as if someone spoke for me" comes from an undated entry in one of Weston's daybooks.

"Nowhere is the where we were —"
Weston was poor enough and cold enough, at one point, to have to convert his glass negatives into windowpanes. I am imagining that some of these held images of Modotti.

"But in that wash of the loss of us —"
The phrase "the pattern will be clearer to us I think after" comes from a letter by Maud Gonne, written after W. B. Yeats's death.

"This dusk makes me think less of you —"
"Eye of the adulterer watches for dusk" comes from Job 24:15: "The eye of the adulterer waits for the twilight, saying, 'No eye will see me.' And he disguises his face."

"Your blank look was too much a mask —"
The phrase "the face of fetishization" comes from my misreading "the fact of fetishization" in a PDF of Laura Mulvey's "Visual Pleasure and Narrative Cinema." Mulvey's work helped me to imagine this poem's frame: Weston confronting, and in some sense paying for, his gaze.

"We were never in the same nation —"
During their years together in Mexico, Weston and Modotti were part of a group that included Diego Rivera and Frida Kahlo. They went to the bull-fights, of which Weston seemed to like writing detailed descriptions, but not taking pictures.

"These lights I live by:"
"You wanted facts, not sighs" inverts a line from W. H. Auden's "Letter to Lord Byron."

"The roses in your picture hold no core —"
This poem refers to Modotti's 1924 photo "Roses, Mexico" and draws some inspiration from Weston's and Modotti's working relationship.

"There are no years or hours —"
"Love is making artificial objects — tools to make tools" misquotes French philosopher Henri Bergson.

"Your form —"
The description of the cypress draws on Weston's photograph "Cypress, Point Lobos."

"She's the image you are but far more —"
Weston's daybooks include more than one description of the movies that he went to see, not as detailed as this, but not far from it.

"A photograph is not a ghost or past —"
Weston cast each of his wives as Eve, in photos that come before and after his iconic work.

"Sex was a lead lens —"
Modotti was deported from Mexico in 1929 for her political work.

"This nude will be seen as the true you —"
This description comes from the photograph "Tina on the Azotea, 1923." Weston and Modotti shared a hacienda in Mexico, and this became some kind of amalgam of home and a place to work, like Weston's other homes, at other times.

"You loved the tragedy factory of me —"
At the beginning, I'm stealing and revising Larry Levis's title, "My Story in a Late Style of Fire." Further in, the narrative centers around Weston's loss of his mother, where he focused on the eye: he wrote to his son that he remembered her eyes "burning with fever," and he went from that into thinking about the art of sight as something preserved.

"Memory will be remade by our art —"
Great writing — by Susan Sontag, Nancy West, and others — has been done about photography's shaping of memory and identity.

"The savior who was yours before me —"
Modotti's first husband was the reason she first went to Mexico; he had moved there and she followed, only to find him dying of smallpox. Diego Rivera included Tina Modotti in at least one painting, in the manner that I describe.

"Stay my gaze —"
After being deported from Mexico, Modotti was not allowed to enter her native Italy and had to settle in Germany instead.

"Your star-dark look —"
Weston wrote in his daybook about going with Modotti to at least one El Dia de los Muertos party dressed as each other.

Acknowledgments

Earlier versions of several of these poems have appeared or are forthcoming in several journals: "You loved the tragedy factory of me —" in *Agni*; "This nude will be seen as the true you" (as "Nude on the Azotea") in *The Laurel Review*; "Nowhere is the where we were," "But in that wash of the loss of us," "Your blank look was too much a mask," "We were never in the same nation," and "There are no years or hours" in *Life and Legends*; "This dusk makes me think less of you" (as "Dusk") in *Memorious*; "Tina mia" in *Pleiades*; and "It was never a matter of aperture" (as "Aperture") in *Southern Humanities Review*.

Natasha Trethewey was kind enough to point me to Margaret Gibbons's *Memories of the Future: The Daybooks of Tina Modotti*, and to help start this whole line of lyric questioning with her own book *Bellocq's Ophelia*. Others whose work and guidance have been essential are Ed Brunner, Rodney Jones, Allison Joseph, Judy Jordan, Aliki Barnstone, and Amy Conger.

Other books from Tupelo Press

Fasting for Ramadan: Notes from a Spiritual Practice (memoir), Kazim Ali
Another English: Anglophone Poems from Around the World (anthology),
   edited by Catherine Barnett and Tiphanie Yanique
Pulp Sonnets (poems, with drawings by Amin Mansouri), Tony Barnstone
Moonbook and Sunbook (poems), Willis Barnstone
gentlessness (poems), Dan Beachy-Quick
Everything That Is Broken Up Dances (poems), James Byrne
New Cathay: Contemporary Chinese Poetry (anthology),
   edited by Ming Di
Calazaza's Delicious Dereliction (poems), Suzanne Dracius,
   translated by Nancy Naomi Carlson
Gossip and Metaphysics: Russian Modernist Poetry and Prose
   (anthology), edited by Katie Farris, Ilya Kaminsky, and Valzhyna Mort
The Posthumous Affair (novel), James Friel
Entwined: Three Lyric Sequences (poems), Carol Frost
Poverty Creek Journal (lyric memoir), Thomas Gardner
The Faulkes Chronicle (novel), David Huddle
Darktown Follies (poems), Amaud Jamaul Johnson
Dancing in Odessa (poems), Ilya Kaminsky
A God in the House: Poets Talk About Faith (anthology), edited by
   Ilya Kaminsky and Katherine Towler
Lucky Fish (poems), Aimee Nezhukumatathil
The Infant Scholar (poems), Kathy Nilsson
Ex-Voto (poems), Adélia Prado, translated by Ellen Doré Watson
Mistaking Each Other for Ghosts (poems), Lawrence Raab
Intimate: An American Family Photo Album (hybrid memoir),
   Paisley Rekdal
Thrill-Bent (novel), Jan Richman
The Book of Stones and Angels (poems), Harold Schweizer
Cream of Kohlrabi (stories), Floyd Skloot
The Well Speaks of Its Own Poison (poems), Maggie Smith
The Perfect Life (lyric essays), Peter Stitt
Soldier On (poems), Gale Marie Thompson
Swallowing the Sea (essays), Lee Upton
Lantern Puzzle (poems), Ye Chun

See our complete list at www.tupelopress.org